Roundy & Friends
Book Six

Andres Varela

Illustrations and Graphic Design by Carlos F. González
Co-Producer Germán Hernández
Fourth Edition
© 2019 Soccertowns® LLC

Previously...

Houston

Kansas City

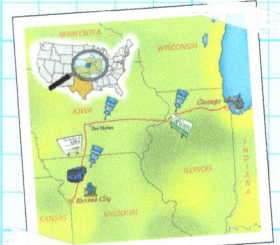

Chicago

Columbus

Washington D.C.

The team has been travelling from Houston to Kansas City, to Chicago, to Columbus, to Washington D.C, and are now arriving in Philadelphia.

They arrive at a Hostel in Downtown Philadelphia. Hostels are places that provide accommodation at an affordable price. They usually provide bunk beds in dormitories, social areas, shared bathrooms and some even offer small kitchens.

While in the hostel the team meets people from all over the world. There are people from the United States, Australia, China, Brazil and Russia.
Can you point out those countries on the following map?
While you think about the answer, Teo is showing some maps to the team.

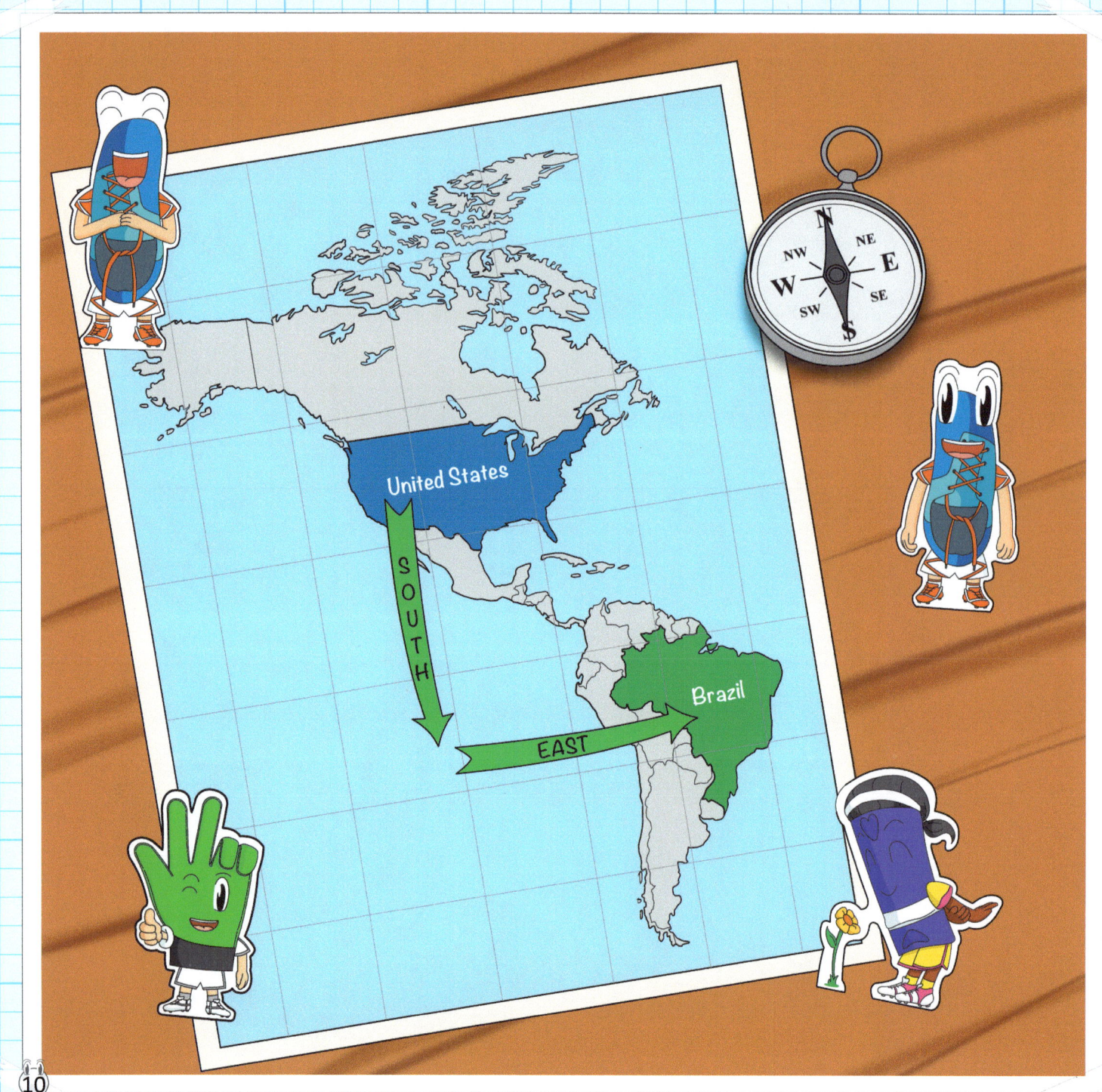

"What are those arrows on the top right of the map?" Asks Roundy.

Teo responds: "Those are the cardinal points or cardinal directions, which are more commonly known just as directions. They help people get to different places."

"How do they help people?" says Emma.

"For example after looking at the map we know that Brazil is South East of the United States. We know this because we followed the South arrow down and then the East arrow over to Brazil. South then East equals South East"

"That is interesting", says Gabe.

Can you tell us what direction Australia is from China?

How about Russia from Australia?

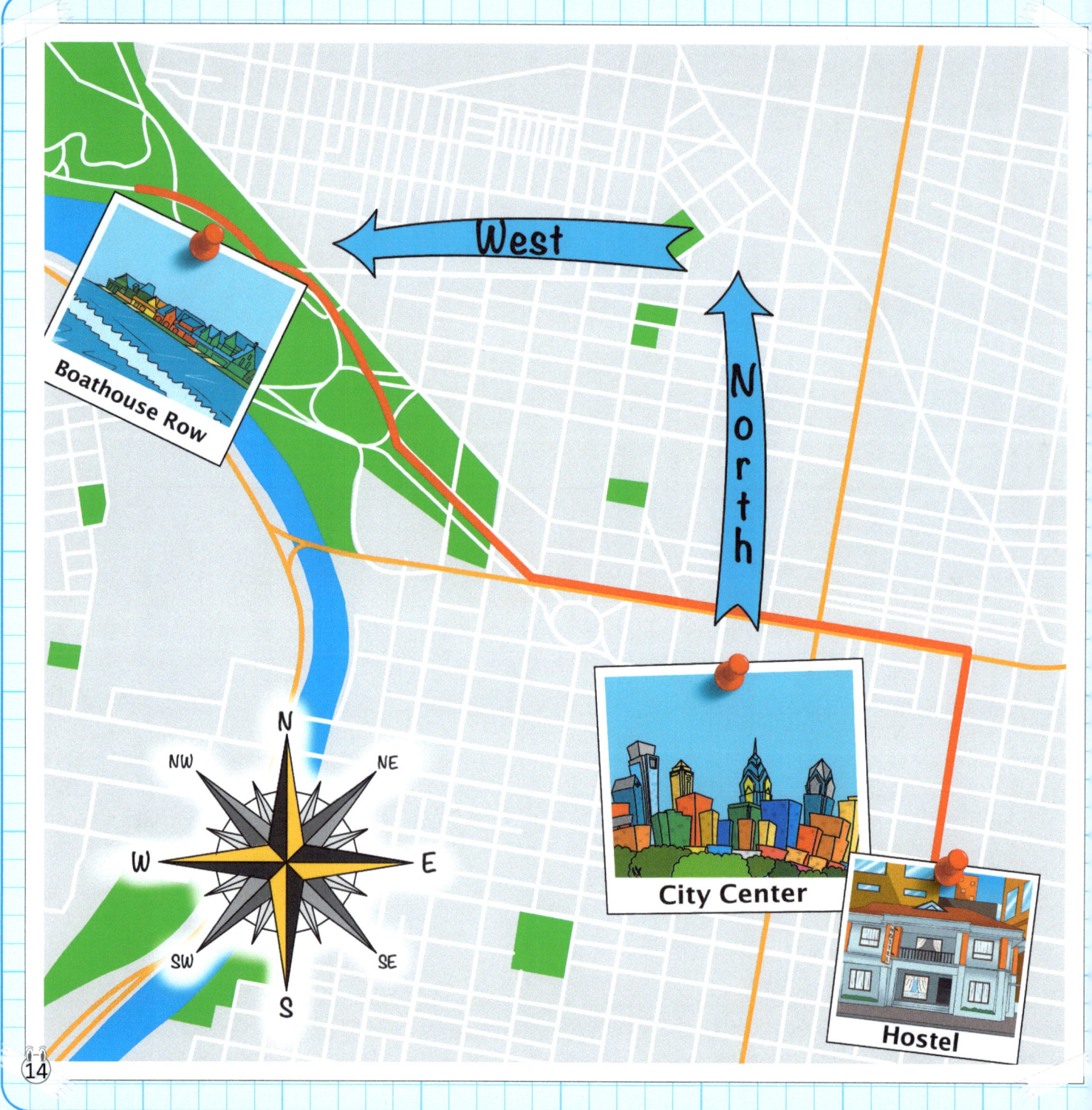

After the team learned how to follow the cardinal directions, they looked at a map and decided they wanted to visit several places in Philadelphia.
They start with a National Historic Landmark called Boathouse Row, which is a very beautiful place with rowing clubs. Boathouse Row is located along the Schuylkill River.
In order to get from the Hostel to Boathouse Row the team needs to go in the North West direction, they get in the car and start their day trip.

The next stop after Boathouse Row is the Liberty Bell Center. The Liberty Bell was originally cast in 1752, that means it was built hundreds of years ago. The Liberty Bell is a symbol of American Independence. In its earlier days the Bell was used to bring politicians together so they could make governmental decisions.

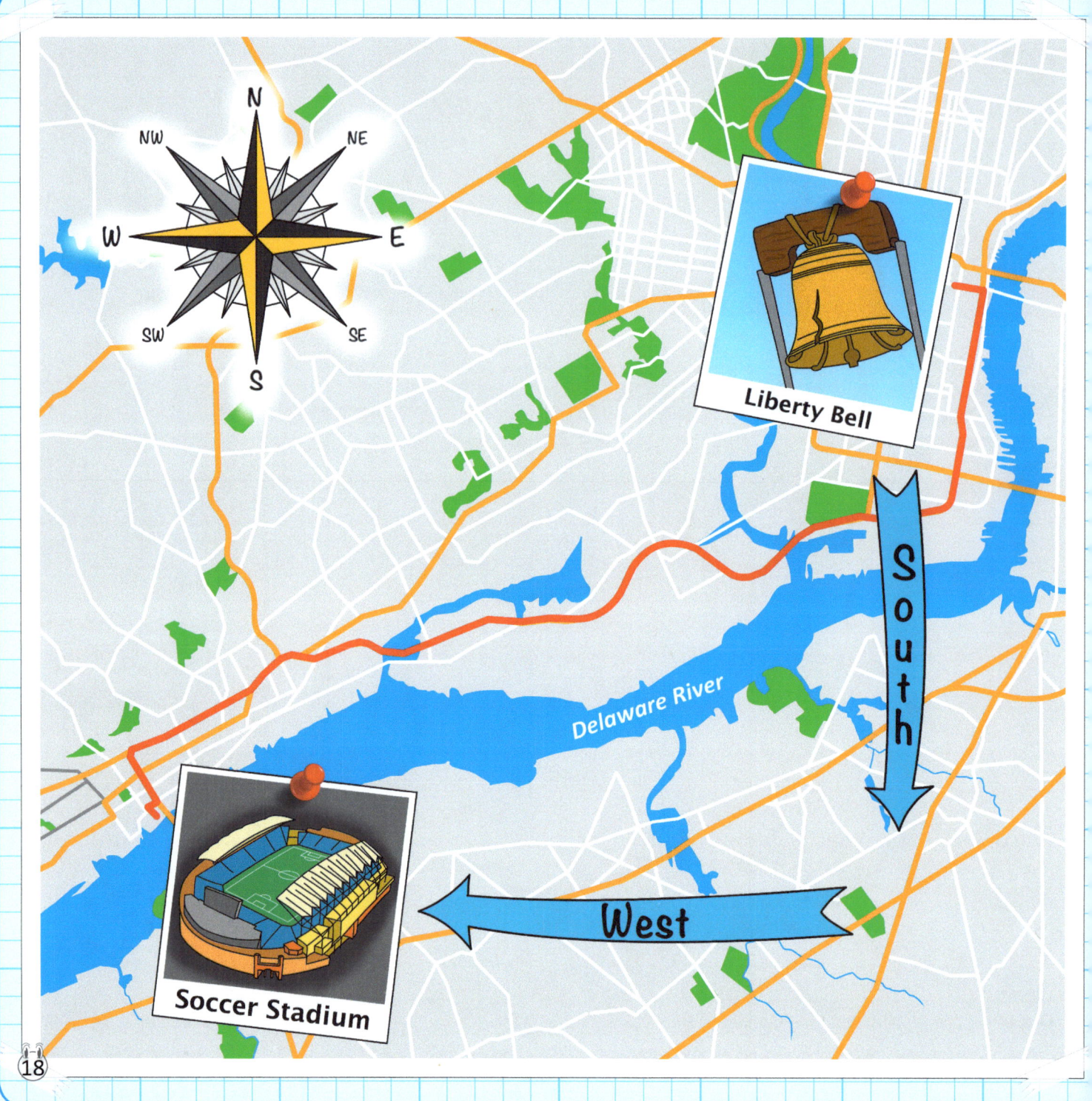

After the Liberty Bell they head in the South West direction towards the Union Soccer Stadium.

They enter the stadium to watch a friendly match. The view from the stands of the stadium is spectacular! They can see the Delaware River. The stadium is located in the State of Pennsylvania and on the other side of the river is the State of New Jersey. The bridge above the river is called the Commodore Barry Bridge.
The bridge was built in the early 1970s and opened to the public on February of 1974. On average there are 35,000 vehicles crossing the bridge every day.

Philadelphia is famous for the Philly Cheese steak, which is basically a sandwich made of a small loaf of bread, thinly sliced beef, onions, peppers and cheese. It is said that a couple from Philadelphia who traditionally sold hot dogs invented the sandwich in the 1930s.
The team loved the Philly Cheese Steaks!

After having some fun at the stadium it is time to move on to the next destination, they head out of Pennsylvania crossing into New Jersey on the Commodore Barry Bridge.

While in Philadelphia the team learned about Cardinal Directions and also about some of the countries that make up our big world, like Brazil, Russia, China and Australia.

Philadelphia taught them a lot of history and introduced them to some great food. Now it's time to get to know another Soccer Town! How about New York City?

We'll see you at the Big Apple!

www.ingramcontent.com/pod-product-compliance
Lightning Source LLC
Chambersburg PA
CBHW040731150426
42811CB00063B/1571